Bipolar C

A Guide to Understanding F
Managing its Triggers to Regain a Sense or
Control and to Live an Emotionally Complete Life
With Supportive Relationships

By Nathan Weaver

Contents

Thank you for buying this book and I hope that you will find it useful. If you will want to share your thoughts on this book, you can do so by leaving a review on the Amazon page, it helps me out a lot.

Introduction

Bipolar is a condition that wreaks havoc on people it impacts. If you struggle with Bipolar, odds are high that your household suffers with you. No matter if you are that member of the family attempting to find out how to cope or you are the individual that has actually been diagnosed, there is hope.

Even though there is no remedy for Bipolar, right now, there are numerous ways in which you may enhance your odds of living a satisfying and long life. The bright side is that the process does not need to be tough either.

The downs and ups are what creates the most issues for people. Being joyful and go lucky one moment is fantastic; however, when it is followed by major lows and depressed moods the following moment, there's a lot more to fret about.

In this book, you are going to discover a variety of different situations that are going to help you to eventually find out how to deal with bipolar and all of these downs and ups. With an understanding of your condition along with assistance in handling the beneficial tools you are going to learn about, you are going to have the ability to improve the lifestyle that your loved ones and you share.

Chapter 1: Understanding Bipolar

Many people that struggle with bipolar have one objective. That objective is to live a life that is as regular as it could be. To make it through the day without having any psychological issues, to make it through the huge conference at work without having individuals question what is wrong and to just have the ability to enjoy your child's graduation are all extra objectives which you might have.

Before you can completely learn to manage bipolar, you have to completely comprehend your condition. You want to understand what things take place, as ideally that you are able to, to ensure that you can then make your coping systems work for you.

There is no one hundred percent certain method of stopping these things from occurring to you. However, there are many things you can find out how to do to aid you in enhancing your outlook.

To get there, we are going to begin by offering you all of the information you require regarding your condition so that you may much better comprehend what is occurring to you. If you are a member of the family who simply wishes to help somebody with bipolar, then, indeed, you too can discover all that you have to so as to provide the assistance that you can offer to them.

The Medical Side

Bipolar is a problem wherein there are extremes in life experiences and moods. There is no uncertainty that bipolar is a health condition that is disabling and severe to those who possess it. It is a mental disorder and it does call for the required treatment.

You might have heard of bipolar being referred to as Manic Depression and that an individual struggling with it has a manic depressive condition. However, what researchers have actually come to discover is that manic style behavior is just one extreme of this condition. The other component of it is the depression. Both of these conditions are extremely major to your health and even to your life expectancy and need to be dealt with.

While medical professionals do not have a bipolar cause, they are working on discovering one. In addition to that, you can be certain that there are numerous researchers trying to find a way to treat the condition. Yet, up until that takes place, we have to analyze what we do understand regarding bipolar and what it does to the individual that you are.

For many people, bipolar begins when they are simply in their teens. Some think that it is activated by adolescence. Others are not going to establish this condition up until they find themselves in their early adult years. Bipolar might last your whole life, as well.

For the majority of people, bipolar does not take place constantly. You do not go in and out of experiences or moods within instants and you do not do this constantly as well. For instance, some individuals are going to have bouts that last for numerous weeks. Others are going to have them for a couple of months. Even though it is feasible to have bipolar wherein your signs flare constantly, this is truly the uncommon case.

If you do not get assistance for bipolar, your condition is most likely to keep on intensifying. There is no question that depression in itself is deadly. For that reason, not getting assistance is just not an option. However, the bright side is that there are treatments, medications and therapies that can aid to minimize the signs and aid you to deal with your condition.

How to Know If You Have Bipolar?

The initial question which you want to ask wheter if you have this condition. Discovering the symptoms and signs is going to aid you to weigh the requirement to look for medical attention. If any of your signs are extreme or you are thinking about hurting yourself, you need to look for medical attention immediately.

Bipolar people are going to go through an alternating sequence of lows and highs that pull on their feelings. The highs are referred to as mania episodes.

The lows are depression episodes. The strength of these lows and highs are going to differ from one person to another and from one episode to the following one. For some, the signs could be rather moderate, but for others, they could be rather extreme. Along with this, you might likewise have really ordinary times as well.

Throughout the manic stage, there are a variety of signs that could be observed.

- You might feel exceptionally positive and pleased. You might feel ecstasy. You might likewise have pumped up self-confidence or ego, as well.

- You might have really bad judgment, and you might understand this by being informed by others that you've made the incorrect choice.

- Your speech could be really quick. Your mind is going bananas with ideas. You might be upset and feel the requirement to move your mind and body. Physical activity might be increased, as well.

- Many are going to be aggressive in their conduct, frequently more so than is "allowed.".

- Some individuals discover this to be a time of issues with sleeping and issues with focusing on what you need to be doing. You might be quickly sidetracked, and have issues getting tasks done.

- You could be careless or you might take chances on things which you generally would not do.

Those that experience the mania part of bipolar are going to shift from it into the depressive side. The depressive side is the one which individuals typically associate with depression-like signs. These signs could consist of the following.

The depressive bipolar signs consist of:

- Feeling really unfortunate, extremely guilty or like everything is lost. Despondence is a typical sensation here as well. The hallmark of an issue is that the signs are inconsistent and unproven.

- You might be extremely exhausted, frequently not caring about getting your tasks completed. You might lose interest in the important things which you do every day, generally. Even those things that you adore doing might not be carried out.

- You might be really irritable, losing your mood for no genuine reason.

- You might not have the ability to sleep even though you are tired. You might not be hungry and some are going to drop weight due to not eating appropriately.

- Some have issues with pain, as well. In case you have pain that there is no genuine cause for, this could be an indication of depressive behavior.

- The most major of all signs and symptoms of depressive behavior is that of ideas of suicide. In case you have these ideas, your condition requires urgent attention.

If you believe that you have any of these signs, then you want to collaborate with your medical professional to be diagnosed. It is essential to receive treatment!

What Causes It?

The one thing that all bipolar individuals wish to know is why. Why did this occur to me? Why do I experience this? Why can't my life be ordinary?

Regrettably, there simply is not a response to that. Neither medical professionals nor researchers comprehend what or why triggers bipolar. However, they have certain ideas regarding what might be behind the way you feel.

Many think that it is a mix of elements that cause this condition, such as genes, environmental and biological elements. Medical professionals think that these conditions not just trigger the bipolar onset in individuals but additionally control when the episodes which you experience take place and how often.

Those with bipolar have issues inside the brain. There are chemical messengers within your brain that go between the brain and the nerve cells. These are referred to as neurotransmitters.

In those who come with bipolar, those messengers are in some way different and merely interact differently with the brain activating the signs that you deal with.

It is thought that those that struggle with bipolar have a hereditary code that places them in that position. While this hereditary disposition does not in itself really set off the condition to transpire, those that have this coding really have a greater likelihood of establishing it eventually in their lives.

This distinction in the neurotransmitters is thought to have to do with an irregular aspect of the genes. Your genes which manage the neurotransmitters in your brain merely established abnormally, resulting in bipolar. However, keep in mind, even if this holds true, it does not indicate that you will experience bipolar. It simply indicates that it is a thing which you might experience.

Along with this hereditary code, a lot of medical professionals think that it is required for you to have some environmental impacts take place so as to set off the issue. This could involve such things as substance abuse and really demanding occasions. In some cases, a really distressing occasion, particularly those that are mental can set off bipolar.

Are You At Risk?

You might be at risk for bipolar in case you have a family bipolar history or additional depressive conditions. Actually, in as much as 90 percent of those with bipolar there is proof of familiar depression.

Once again, in case you have genes passed down from those in your family with these problems, then you have higher odds of experiencing bipolar. While the precise genes are not known right now, there are lots of scientists working on discovering the gene which makes you more or less prone to bipolar.

Should You Call a Doctor?

If you read this far, then you most likely recognize the significance of looking for medical attention. The issue is that many that have signs of bipolar do not understand that they do have an issue.

Some are going to understand that something is wrong; however, most are not going to recognize simply how impaired they are. Additionally, many do not understand simply how problematic going through these mood swings could be for other members of the family. You most likely do not recognize what you are placing your friends and family through.

For that reason, it frequently takes another person, like your partner, buddy or other relatives to aid you to get to the medical professional so that you could be diagnosed for your own well-being and health. Those who are worried about their loved ones need to look for the assistance that they require. Professional assistance could be rather beneficial to those who are suffering.

If an individual that is struggling with bipolar does not look for and get the assistance that he or she requires, not just are stresses going to continue to develop, however, physical issues could additionally end up being obvious. They could be injured in one of their episodes.

Who Should I Contact?

If you recognize the requirement to look for professional assistance, your initial contact ought to be your family physician. He or she can assist you in establishing that there are no other medical issues triggering your condition. From here, however, the individual to see is a psychiatrist.

Do not fret; the procedure of looking for assistance in handling any kind of mental disorder, including bipolar syndrome and depression is rather uncomplicated. Take a loved one with you who has actually seen the signs which you are experiencing. The initial thing that your medical professional is going to ask is what kind of signs you are having. He or she is going to ask you to explain both the depressive signs and the mania signs.

Throughout your initial conference with the medical professional, you'll discuss your everyday life, the episodes you are experiencing and your total health. The initial thing that he or she is going to do is work on dismissing other medical issues and other psychological health issues. Other conditions, like mood disorders, schizophrenia, attention deficit hyperactivity disorder, and even a personality disorder, could have comparable signs to bipolar.

Your medical professional might likewise ask you to go through tests that are going to identify if there are any other things which are triggering your condition. He or she is going to wish to discover if you have physical causes.

This could consist of discussing substance abuse. Your medical professional is going to ask and require a truthful opinion about this. If you consume alcohol, utilize illegal drugs like cocaine and cannabis, then you have to inform your medical professional about these. Keep in mind, your medical professional can't talk about this with anybody else. These kinds of drugs could change the mood, and in some individuals, produce bigger mood fluctuations.

Another feasible reason for your state of mind swings could be because of health issues such as thyroid disorders. Here, a blood test is going to be needed. It is going to evaluate how well your thyroid is functioning. Many who have mood swings really have an underactive thyroid. The bright side is that if this is the issue, there are medications which are able to treat thyroid issues.

Still, there is more to discuss with your medical professional. You'll wish to inform him about the meds which you are taking, as these could additionally trigger a lot of mood swings. For instance, medications such as corticosteroids consisting of prednisone could trigger mood swings. In case you are being treated for anxiety with meds, or for anxiety, then your medication could cause mood swings. The medications that are utilized to deal with Parkinson's disease are additionally mood swing susceptible medications.

Your medical professional is going to ask you about your eating plan, as well. Those who are deficient in B 12 vitamins, particularly, could experience large mood swings.

Any of these kinds of conditions could lead your physician to ascertain that you are struggling with bipolar disorder. By talking with you and taking a look at the test results, your physician is able to identify precisely what is happening with you.

It is extremely crucial for you to communicate with your physician about any of your requirements and to be sincere regarding your condition. By telling them about your regular life, involving the bad parts, he or she is able to make the appropriate decisions to assist with treating your conditions.

It is most likely that you are going to find that your physician is rather experienced in bipolar. That's since each year countless individuals see their physicians with worry about having this condition. It is not as unusual as you might believe!

As soon as this has actually been carried out, your physician and you can work on a therapy for your condition.

Chapter 2: Why Bother Getting Help?

Bipolar is a mental disorder. It is not a thing like a cold that is going to vanish. It is not like a leg that is broken, which is going to recover by itself. Without professional attention, your bipolar can and is going to worsen.

What occurs to you is going to be unique. There is no method of understanding if your condition is going to intensify rapidly or whatsoever. However, research reveals that those who do not look for assistance for their condition are going to discover problems that do exist for them and for their loved ones.

In case you have bipolar, other conditions may make it even worse. For instance, if you are attempting to deal with depression, you are going to have a difficult time doing so due to bipolar. In conditions where this is deadly, for instance, if you are struggling with alcoholism, this could be a really major issue.

If you can't stay away from alcohol, then your life might be in jeopardy. Not just is the alcohol going to cause issues for your health, yet bipolar could make you think irrationally and you might put yourself in harmful circumstances. Because of this, looking for assistance is a necessity.

For certain people, the duration of time in between manic and depressive signs could be really brief. You might move from one sign to the next rapidly, causing confusion and even health scares. This quick cycling is going to cause you a fair bit of sorrow.

It could get even worse, as well. It is feasible, trust it or not, to be in a state of depression along with a mania simultaneously. When this takes place, the end outcome is that your mind and feelings are entirely wrapped in one other. You are irritated and upset. You are not able to eat or sleep. You can't get your thoughts to be arranged.

Even worse, when this occurs, individuals are more likely to consider suicide. This could be really detrimental due to the fact that individuals in this frame of mind are not thinking reasonably whatsoever and could make a bad decision.

Another issue is that of psychosis. Bipolar signs which blend both depression and mania signs could cause psychosis. This is a really major mental disorder in which your personality is entirely disordered. You are impaired with what is real and what isn't. You are delusional and hallucinating. Even those who really firmly believe in stuff could wind up making decisions the other way.

The Stress Goes Further

Even beyond the physical risks which you put yourself beneath when you deal with bipolar, there are just as destructive impacts it has on your relationships.

Lots of people with bipolar are going to have difficulty holding onto relationships. They might move from one person to another rapidly due to the mood swings which they deal with. Additionally, those that are struggling with bipolar frequently make errors in dealing with other people. They merely are puzzled as to what the true emotion ought to be throughout any such circumstances.

Along with this, many with bipolar additionally have financial issues too. They do not make the appropriate decisions concerning cash, spending on credit and making purchasing decisions. With this comes a manner of issues, from needing to file bankruptcy to having to burden other members of the family with this issue.

In some cases, a mania episode could set off a shopping spree. Or a depressive episode might do the identical only in the wrong way.

Still, one of the most severe impacts of bipolar is the manner in which individuals with it treat themselves. Many discover that the only method to manage what is taking place is to isolate themselves from everybody.

This occurs quickly throughout depressive stages specifically when a person is having an extreme episode. Without the protection they require from a loved one, they can allow their self-destructive ideas to take control. Due to this isolation, it is necessary for those who have family members in this condition to supply them with the care which they require to keep them secure.

As you may observe, the bipolar complications could be rather extreme. Since lots of people who struggle with this condition just do not understand that they have it, it could quickly escalate and even put individuals in danger as they are doing the things which they do each day.

The risk of driving a vehicle, for instance, is quite real. If depressive mood changes or a mania take place, the individual can quickly lose control of the vehicle. Even worse, they might make bad decisions in traffic, placing others in danger in addition to them. This circumstance could be played out with numerous other circumstances in your life as well.

Getting assistance, however, could actually enhance your outlook on life and decrease your complications and risks considerably.

Chapter 3: Bipolar Treatment

As we have actually gone over, the initial thing that you want to do is to talk with your physician to identify what is impacting you. If it is, actually, bipolar disorder, then there are numerous treatment alternatives that your physicians are going to suggest to you.

The procedure of dealing with bipolar is going to come from 2 primary forms, from your physician, that is. The initial requirement is that of medication. The second is that of psychotherapy. The mix of these things has actually worked in helping countless individuals to enhance their lives even while struggling with bipolar.

There is no remedy for bipolar, however, with the appropriate treatments, you could enhance your life quality and keep yourself safe, as well.

It is the mix of both medication and extra psychotherapy assistance that is the most effective path. Later on, we are going to discuss other things that you might do beyond your physician's care that could likewise help in your improvement.

Medications

There are a lot of various medications out there that your physician could prescribe to provide some aid to you. Medications have the objective of aiding to manage your mood swings.

The most typical kinds of medications for mood control consist of Lithium in name brands like Eskalith and Lithobid. These function as mood stabilizers and are really among the initial resources against manic episodes. They are your initial line of defense against your mood swings.

Along with these, there are other meds which are utilized to aid with stabilizing the mood. Anti-seizure medications particularly offer the assistance that's required. These consist of medications such as valproic acid with the brand name of Depakene.

Divalproex, Lamotrigine additionally supply this identical help.

They function as mood regulators. A less frequently utilized anti-seizure medication Topiramate, which is offered as Topamax.

Yet, there is more assistance required in the upkeep of the mood swings caused by bipolar disorder. You most likely are going to deal with episodes of depression and frequently, medical professionals find it essential to deal with these signs meticulously.

They could, in fact, be dealt with in a variety of ways, however. Your physician has a number of ways to go.

He might choose to provide you antidepressants. Antidepressants are perfect for dealing with depression, particularly and for that reason, frequently work with bipolar individuals. These medications include a medication line consisting of:

- Paroxetine (promoted as Paxil)

- Bupropion (promoted as Wellbutrin)

- Fluoxetine (promoted as both Sarafem and Prozac)

- Sertraline (promoted as Zoloft)

Along with these, your physician has the capability to supply you with antipsychotic medications if he considers that you require them. This involves 2 kinds, including olanzapine as Zyprexa and risperidone as Risperdal.

Several medications have actually been produced to deal with both the manic and the depressive signs which you encounter with bipolar disorder. For instance, just recently, the FDA authorized quetiapine as Seroquel to deal with both degrees of your condition.

Yet, there are certain issues about medications which deal with bipolar. There are certain health hazards which you can take on since you are consuming these medications.

The American Diabetes Association has actually performed research on several of these frequently utilized medications and has actually discovered that there are some really severe risks with them. For those who are on antipsychotic meds, the risk that is greatest in the diabetes development.

Additionally, you are susceptible to putting on weight to a really shocking level without the appropriate workout and eating plan. In association with this, the added weight could result in boosts in blood pressure, which places your heart at risk for issues.

This does not suggest that you can't take these meds if your physician tells you to. As a matter of fact, you need to take them if your physician tells you to due to the fact that they could enhance your health and life. However, you ought to constantly follow the suggestions of your physician in regards to constraints in addition to exercise and diet.

Several medications, such as Risperdal, Seroquel and Zyprexa are just utilized in extreme bipolar conditions. Even then, your physician is going to carefully monitor your health in use of them and doing this aids to keep complication risks at bay even when you consume this medication frequently as you are going to for bipolar.

Every medication which you take is going to have different side effects and responses. Certain individuals discover that medications provide no side effects to them while the identical medication taken by somebody else is going to have extreme side effects.

When taking these medications for the initial time, it is important for you to think about how they impact you. If you discover that they are overwhelming or merely offer too serious side effects, then call your physician immediately so that he may modify the dose.

Additionally, you ought to understand that medications frequently require some time in your system before you'll really see any outcomes. Certain medications could require weeks before you discover their full benefit.

If it goes this long and you do not see any kind of enhancement, speak with your physician. There ought to be another medication that is going to provide the wanted results.

It is going to take a while before your physician is going to have the ability to get the right dosage for you. Be patient and collaborate with your physician as carefully as you can to really get the benefits that you can have.

Psychotherapy

Even though psychotherapy seems like a quite scary thing, it is, in fact, something that could be performed quickly and with your assistance, it could be rather enjoyable for you.

Throughout psychotherapy, your physician and you are going to work together to identify the most effective treatment for you. Typically, you'll be taking medications throughout this procedure. The mix could be rather beneficial to your total health.

By consulting with a physician to discuss psychotherapy, you both could find out more about your bipolar condition. The objective is going to be to discover patterns in your episodes. By tracking and looking into the pattern of episodes that you undergo, your physician can better comprehend what activates them.

By tracking your mood alterations, the physician can notice if there is anything that triggers them, to begin with. For instance, if you take medications for some other problem, those meds might really be activating your mood alterations and resulting in the impact of bipolar.

Other typical triggers consist of feelings. For instance, if you have a disagreement with a loved one that is intense, then you might experience a mood swing that is extreme. Along with psychological causes, physical changes could additionally activate your causes.

Simply recognizing these patterns is inadequate, though. Throughout psychotherapy, your physician is going to work on discovering ways for you to handle these episodes. By knowing to manage the uncertainties which bipolar raises, you could enhance your general well being.

Medication by itself does seldom bring the aid that you'll require to handle bipolar disorder. Those that encounter this condition have to discover how to recognize that they are dealing with mood swings. Psychotherapy could enable them to recognize that they are able to deal with what's occurring to them and stop harming themselves and people around them.

It could even assist you in understanding the significance of carrying on with your medications. When you understand the degree of what you do throughout your mood swings and how they are misguided, you could learn to identify them and you'll understand that you require medication to assist with managing them as much as feasible.

Psychotherapy is a thing you ought to do on a continuing basis. By accomplishing this, you enable yourself to obtain the most assistance that you can have.

Electroconvulsive Therapy

For those who have extreme bipolar disorder, psychotherapy and medications might not suffice to supply them with the alleviation that they require. Electroconvulsive therapy is another option that is out there for you. You are going to hear about it being referred to as ECT more frequently.

Those who have electroconvulsive therapy usually have not reacted well from the medications which have actually been utilized to assist them. Additionally, they usually have very serious depression in which suicidal ideas are frequent. In instances where suicidal tendencies are observed, it could be crucial to look for extra treatment.

In electroconvulsive therapy, your physician is going to utilize electrodes put on your head to begin the treatment. Your physician is going to likewise provide you a muscle relaxer throughout the treatment. When this is finished, you are going to be provided anesthesia and you will not feel a thing.

As soon as this is done, the electrodes are going to deliver an extremely tiny quantity of electrical current. As the current travels through your brain, your brain is going to really have a seizure. While in regular conditions, a brain seizure could be very serious and traumatic, not does that occur here.

Since you have taken a muscle relaxant, your body remains calm and still. The current just goes through your brain for less than a moment.

However, why is this performed? There are really very few answers to that question! Throughout the procedure of electro convulsion, your brain is going to respond in a really special way. Your brain's metabolic process changes considerably. The manner in which blood streams through your brain additionally changes. The end outcome is that the depression you deal with is minimized substantially and you feel much better.

Even though this has actually been shown to aid relieve depression and depression signs in cases like bipolar disorder, it is not totally comprehended why this takes place.

It could appear really problematic to attempt this treatment. Besides, it does not sound like passing an electrical current through your brain is an advantageous thing.

However, keep in mind that the quantity of current and the time in which it enters the brain are really, really tiny. That combined with the muscle relaxer control, you wind up gaining from it rather than enduring it.

What Should You Do?

Although numerous kinds of treatment for bipolar are listed here, it is going to be up to you and your physician to identify what the best strategy is for you. This choice is going to originate from your condition and its intensity.

It is additionally going to take a while to change medications and to notice psychotherapy benefits. Throughout that time, you might not have the ability to see much enhancement. Yet, research studies have actually revealed benefits in the mix of psychotherapy and medications enough so that numerous individuals see an amazing improvement in their regular lives.

By collaborating with your physician, you too, may discover this benefit. Yet, it is going to be essential for you to do simply that: collaborate with your physician. Remain in continuous interaction with him about how you are doing. He exists to help work out the wrinkles to discover the most effective option for you.

However, is that all? Is that all the assistance that you could obtain for your condition? No, and that is why this guide is just halfway finished. There are other manners in which you could learn to manage your condition.

Chapter 4: Why Is Treatment So Hard For Many People

Even though psychotherapy and medication are approaches for handling bipolar disorder, oftentimes, people merely are not going to take them. They stop. They quit. They just can not stand the whole procedure of battling their minds and bodies. They simply quit.

As you can most likely imagine, this is just not the most effective path for you to take when it pertains to taking care of your condition. Yet, a large number of bipolar disorder individuals are going to experience this feeling eventually.

Mood stabilizers and antipsychotic medications are frequently the kinds of medications with the most side effects and for that reason, the most typically stopped by the individual.

Yet, those that simply stop taking these medications against their physician's suggestions frequently deal with a substantial issue. They relapse in their signs. They are typically hospitalized. They wind up homeless, victims, and even are more typically involved in numerous kinds of criminal activity. Either in jail or in a medical facility, those who do not have the meds they require wind up in trouble.

Noncompliance

When an individual stops taking their medication, this is referred to as noncompliance or often it is referred to as nonadherence. It is not simply those who experience bipolar and take these meds that encounter this issue.

Actually, those who are informed they have to take meds for extended time periods frequently go through a bout of not wishing to do so any more. Those that struggle with high blood pressure, epilepsy and even asthma frequently face this sensation of wishing to stop the meds.

One thing to comprehend is that you do not need to quit taking all of your meds to deal with an issue. Some people just stop taking a few of them; possibly those which they still have pills available for, and stop others. Partial noncompliance is equally as troublesome as those that deal with cutting off all meds completely.

However, this does not address our concern of why this occurs. Regrettably, there are a variety of different reasons why it is going to occur.

You Do Not Understand Your Condition

The initial and most typical reason that this takes place is just since individuals do not comprehend the illness that they are dealing with. Actually, some 10 out of 14 clients are going to quit taking medications since they do not understand how essential they are to their illness.

Lots of patients, approximately 80 percent, are going to take meds just due to the fact that their physicians tell them to. Lots do not recognize why they have to take the meds which they do, yet merely do so since their physician tells them to. Due to the fact that individuals do this, it is tough to understand simply how conscious they are of their illness.

Among the most essential things that you may do, then, is to genuinely understand your problem. If your family member is suffering from a bipolar, then assist them to remain informed about their problem. It is necessary that you offer this information due to the fact that, without it, they might not understand the significance of taking those pills every day.

With this education, however, protection could be substantial from these issues.

Dependency

Even though the absence of awareness regarding their condition is the single most prevalent reason which individuals do not take their meds, the dependency they have on drugs and alcohol is an additional reason why it occurs.

Those who place themselves in this position are at high risk of health-related issues as a result of those meds. A lot of times, it ends up being really essential for an individual to choose. Should they take the meds or should they keep on doing drugs or consume alcohol?

This choice is frequently one that takes place since psychiatrists frequently inform their clients that they can't take their meds and drink simultaneously. This, in itself, is an extremely damaging mix. Mixing drugs or alcohol with your medications could have extreme health consequences.

Instead of choosing not to do drugs or drink, the dependency that numerous bipolar individuals have towards these compounds keeps them consuming those rather than medications. This could be really damaging to their well-being, however.

Due to this, it is vital that individuals couple medical treatment with substance abuse treatment simultaneously so as to stop themselves from these kinds of circumstances which could eventually result in a health crisis.

They Do Not Like The Physician

Another reason why certain bipolar individuals quit taking their medications is as easy as they simply do not like their psychiatrist. While this could be noted as a reason for not heading to the physician as you ought to, you must never ever quit taking your meds because of this.

If you do not like your psychiatrist or physician for whichever reason, look for the assistance of another one. The relocation is uncomplicated and the end outcome is that you have the care which you require without risking your medication use.

Side Effects

Even though lots of people think that the medication side effects are the reason why numerous individuals stop taking their bipolar medications, studies have actually revealed that this is not nearly as crucial as the absence of understanding of their illness. Nonetheless, 10 percent of individuals are going to quit taking medications due to the side effects connected with them.

The issue here is not that the medication is too severe for you. The issue is not that the medication is the incorrect one for you. The issue is that your dose might be bad. Too low or high of a dosage could cause a variety of severe side effects. Collaborating with your physician, you may get this dose right so that you enhance your general benefits.

It is frequent to hear that medications which are taken initially, referred to as the first-generation antipsychotics, are frequently more susceptible to side effects than those which are taken when the initial generation does not work. Medications such as Abilify and Seroquel, Geodon and Zyprexa typically have less side effects than other meds.

Hereof, then, certain physicians are going to alter the medication which you are taking if they identify that the side effects you are dealing with are that serious.

If you talk with your physician, you could quickly discover the appropriate medication for your requirements as well as for your side effect magnitude. By overcoming the initial couple of months with your physician, the appropriate medication is going to be discovered for your particular case.

What Else Could It Be?

There are lots of other reasons why individuals stop taking their medications. Those who do not see a really fast improvement in their signs do not take them long enough to notice their positive aspects. Certain medications require weeks to, in fact, see a result in their utilization.

Those who struggle with depression, even in simply bouts, additionally typically deal with the issue of not wishing to take their medications because this variable. Those who deal with the depression of any intensity need to have somebody to assist them to remember to take their meds for their personal health.

Certain individuals do not take their medications due to the fact that they do not have them. There is no question that medications are pricey and when you can't pay for them, you do not get them. This issue is one that has to be dealt with by your physician, you and the financial aid which might be available to you via governmental offices.

Lastly, some individuals do not take their bipolar medication merely since they delight in being in their manic phase. Still, this phase is just a phase and you are still placing yourself at risk of health-related disease by not taking your meds!

Chapter 5: Dealing With Bipolar

Among the most significant messages you have to draw from this guide is the truth that you could enhance your condition if you make certain adjustments in your way of life. You could learn to manage bipolar.

You might sit there and think to yourself how you simply do not wish to handle this. You might wish to have the ability to write it off as an "Oh well." However, actually, you've seen reasons why it's not so simple. Now, that you understand that, take the time to understand what modifications you could make in your life to really enhance your general quality of life.

Do not attempt to make all of these adjustments today. Give yourself perseverance and time to overcome every one. Doing so is going to provide you more capability to, in fact, achieve success with handling bipolar disorder.

In this chapter, we discuss a variety of basic manners in which you can enhance your quality of life by knowing coping strategies. Take them one step at a time; however, try to get them all worked into your way of life. They appear straightforward since they could be just that.

How You Sleep

The manner in which you sleep plays a considerable role in your bipolar condition. What is necessary to keep in mind here is that when you sleep in a regular pattern, there are chemical alterations within the brain which are helpful to your problem.

To enhance this condition, merely get ample sleep every night, however, do this by going to sleep around the identical time every night and wake up around the identical time every morning. Developing a pattern such as this is going to enhance your bipolar signs.

If you have a job which has you sleeping at weird times, you want to attempt to figure out a schedule so that even when you aren't working, you are still sleeping at the same times. This is vital to your coping abilities. It additionally provides your mind the time that it requires to clear and to awaken revitalized.

Actually, when you do have to make adjustments in your sleep pattern that are extreme, like a brand-new time zone, speak to your physician about the most effective method to do this without creating issues for yourself.

Track Your Meds

We have actually talked a great deal about medications which you need to take and the reasons behind this. However, you could additionally discover how to manage this process to make it that much more effective.

Take your meds even if you feel fantastic. Do what your physician tells you to when it comes to taking them even when you have no signs. Even if you feel truly great, that's your medication talking and functioning! By stopping the intake of them, you merely enable the signs to start all over.

To make the whole procedure of medication-taking simple, plan your schedule in order to include your dosing. For instance, when you get up in the morning, eat your breakfast and take your morning tablets. In case you take a second tablet later on during the day, do that after supper, for instance. By combining medication taking and meals, for instance, you stop yourself from overlooking them.

In case you do take more than one tablet and are quickly perplexed by them, buy a tablet organizer and utilize this to divvy up your medications. Those which are for a week or perhaps a month at a time are outstanding tools to make sure that you do not forget and do not end up being puzzled with meds.

Another suggestion to bear in mind regarding your meds is that they do not blend well. If you catch a cold, call your physician about what cold medications you could take with your bipolar meds. You ought to never ever blend them with any kind of drugs or alcohol.

If another physician recommended medications for you, do not take them up until you are totally certain that they understand the bipolar meds you are taking. If and when medications are combined, they could interact with one another and even cause severe conditions.

Maintain Your Activity Level

A vital part of handling bipolar disorder is to entirely manage and arrange your life in the ideal way that you are able zo. For those who are accustomed to working really hard, each day, this might indicate dialing that down a bit.

Regardless of what you do, by managing how much you do every day, you additionally aid to alleviate those chemicals in your brain and for that reason, you avoid the signs that could often occur when you are anxiously running around one day and not doing anything except watching tv the following day!

Do Not Utilize Drugs Or Alcohol

The urge to utilize drugs and alcohol is really strong for many individuals. When you are managing the signs of bipolar, you might feel the requirement to simply unwind. Turning to drugs or alcohol could be a big temptation. The mood swings might feel much better while you are drunk. However, the mix of medications with these compounds could be deadly. Some are going to take drugs and alcohol to aid them sleep. The issue is that it generally makes it even worse.

In case you have issues with drugs and alcohol, looking for therapy and assistance is going to aid to give you the strength that you require to conquer this issue. Among the most effective tools to utilize is that of Alcoholics Anonymous or other groups of that kind. We are going to speak more about their features in just a minute.

The utilization of caffeine, alcohol and even over-the-counter medications could be lethal and could trigger enough trouble for you to send you to the medical facility. This is particularly accurate for over-the-counter cold medications and allergic reaction medications. Constantly talk to your physician about the best medications to utilize when you are sick.

Along with that, understand that these nonprescription meds can set off mood swings, even when you are taking the medication.

They could disrupt your sleep patterns, trigger appetite loss and place your body in a vulnerable position. If you end up being ill, speak with your physician about the most effective medications for your problem.

Caffeine provides the identical kind of trigger and stops you from obtaining sleep, as well. In case you feel that you require coffee in the early morning, you want to locate a decaffeinated coffee or quit consuming it altogether. Simply a tiny amount of this kind of item daily is all that it is going to require to restrict the medication effectiveness.

- Do not utilize alcohol

- Do not utilize illegal drugs

- Cut as many caffeine-related items such as soda, chocolate and coffee out of your eating plan.

- Ask your physician which nonprescription medications are fine for you to utilize with your present prescription medications and those that are not going to trigger issues with sleep deprivation and mood swings.

Doing those 4 things could significantly enhance the quality of life you have. Even though it might appear difficult to not have the ability to have a beverage, you understand that the benefits of not needing to handle mood swings matter more.

Support

Obtaining support from your household is essential. Numerous bipolar individuals like to believe that they may do it by themselves. However, as we have actually gone over, it is extremely hard to do this. The majority of the time, you will not recognize how serious your mood swing is. You might not recognize that you are lashing out at a family member without reason.

Step one is to inform those who you love about your disorder. As tough as that seems, those near to you could be your safety net. They could assist you in understanding what is occurring and how you are behaving. A helpful individual are going to direct you to assist and is going to stand by you during this prognosis and this life long difficulty.

Step 2 is to recognize that you aren't the only person who is suffering. Bipolar individuals frequently lash out at the people they love. Those in your household need to handle mood swings that can be rather extreme. Even though you feel you can't do a great deal about this, aiding your loved ones to be informed and educated regarding what is going on is going to minimize the quantity of stress that plays along with bipolar.

If they understand what you are struggling with, they could assist you. If they do not, they do not comprehend why you are doing what you are doing. That causes family tension and unpleasant circumstances. Without an understanding of what is occurring, your family simply can't be as encouraging as they might be otherwise.

Along with simply knowing the impact that bipolar disorder has on you, you ought to additionally look for the assistance that you require from a family therapist. Even a family without a lot of strife in it is going to want to get the support and aid of a therapist. Bipolar disorder creates trauma in families and having this extra assistance is a huge help.

Lastly, when an informed family is able to assist the individual who is struggling with bipolar disorder, he or she could pursue improvement with assistance. The family could offer assistance when mood swings take control.

And, they could aid to keep your physician and you educated about the manner in which you respond to scenarios, to mood swings and even to your medications. That amounts to an effective scenario for the bipolar individual.

A family is a tool that all bipolar individuals require; however, oftentimes you might feel the wish to just run and hide. You might feel as if you would rather be on your own. Making it through that feeling is going to result in success.

Reducing Stress

Simply reading the title of this part you are thinking that you are not able to do it. You have actually heard it previously. You understand that stress is a killer of many individuals, not simply those who experience bipolar. Yet, it is vital that you take a look at your life and recognize those times when stress has caused mood swings or perhaps out of hand behaviors which place you in danger.

If you force yourself at work to be the individual who does the most, what do you achieve? You most likely are going to create the onset of many signs of bipolar, particularly of mood swings. When this takes place, you place yourself in a position of not having the ability to work and, even worse, placing your position in danger.

For that reason, you wind up not really gaining from all of your effort, but rather, have less benefits, and eventually, you drop the performance level that you might have had.

Meanwhile, if you would have worked at a stable schedule and done what you should have done regarding stress management, you eventually would have achieved more.

Here are certain suggestions for stress management at the office.

- Work the identical hours as much as you can. By working a stable and foreseeable schedule, that enables you to stay with a schedule that assists in minimizing mood swings.

- Obtain the rest that you require. You want to attempt to sleep at the identical time every day. You want to be able to track your patterns of sleep to decrease mood swings.

- When you are struggling with mood swings, think about whether you must be working. For certain people, it might suggest talking with your physician about how they impact your job. Eventually, you want to choose if you are benefiting yourself or not by continuing to work and tolerate these mood swings.

- Take some time off. Those who take time off frequently improve their general well being and health. By obtaining time off weekly and even vacation time, (or taking some time off when you have to), you enhance your degree of stress and how the body responds.

- Do not work in excessively demanding environments. While you might not feel that this is a thing that you may manage, it has to be. Those that deal with bipolar disorder have to think about their health above anything else. Mood swings, manic and depressive signs, could be intensified when you place yourself in a situation to handle a great deal of stress.

Work through issues. If there are tiny things that take place that cause you to stress or trigger stress, manage them immediately. Little issues develop into big ones that are much less probable to be handled. By managing issues rapidly, you minimize the stress toll that they take on you eventually.

Lowering stress ought to be among the most crucial things that you do. By doing so, you minimize the danger of having a mood swing due to stress. Find out how to identify demanding circumstances and discover how to leave them successfully! It will pay off.

Watch For Signs

Believe it or not, discovering how to keep an eye out for signs of the beginning of mood swings could be an exceptional tool to help you in dealing with your disease. The early warning indications of an episode could be observed before they end up being full-blown swings.

Why do you wish to actually take notice of this? There are a variety of benefits which could stem from you noticing and acting when you see them.

Regrettably, your physician can just offer you an idea of what is going to take place to you throughout a mood swing. That's since everyone is unique which in itself provides for difficulties. Everyone is going to move from depressive signs to manic signs in a different way and at different times.

The quicker you see that your mood is altering, the quicker you can act to prevent it or at least to handle what is coming. The quicker you do this, the quicker the assistance can reach you.

What are the warning indications? Here are certain things which could be a little mood change that eventually can be a predictor of a big mood swing around the corner. Find out how to see these to identify mood changes.

- Sleep changes. In case you are on a sleep pattern (which you ought to be) when you see that you can not sleep or you are exhausted even after obtaining a complete night's rest, this could be a mood swing predictor.

- Energy level. Changes in energy levels are a powerful sign you are having a mood change. Given that the majority of the time mania is going to include boosted energy while depressive signs reduce it, you could see how this might be identified.

- Sexual interest loss. Some individuals will experience times when they do not desire any kind of sexual touching. Although it is common for individuals to be interested and not interested typically, a change that is substantial ought to be kept in mind.

Focus. You go to work and do the job. In some cases, you might sense that you simply can't remain on task. When you feel that you can't focus and complete the tasks that you began, this could be an indication of a mood change.

- Self-confidence. It is necessary for members of the family to notice these circumstances. If you or your family member determine that you are down and out or you are saying unfavorable things about yourself, then this might be an indication that depressive signs are coming. It is necessary that these things be detected and dealt with immediately.

Thought changes. If you simply for no reason appear to be really positive, or you are thinking of death a great deal, this could be a indication of a mood swing. In case these thoughts become suicidal, it is essential to look for assistance immediately.

- Changes in how you look. Certain bipolar patients are going to undergo phases in which they feel as if they have to alter the manner in which they look. You might alter the manner in which you groom. You might suddenly hate the clothing that you have. These could be signs of a mood swing as a result of the feeling that is typically linked to them.

The early mood swing warning signs could be terrific tools to help you in identifying problems before they take place, or at least to the degree that they can occur. However, among the issues with this is that many people can't detect these things by themselves. They typically see these stresses as simply their regular lifestyle.

Because of this, it is essential that members of the family have the ability to identify these early warning indications and after that help you to make it through them. By identifying changes in you, your family is able to assist you to obtain a bit of help and rapidly!

What should be carried out if you experience a few of these mood changes? If you observe the warning indications, you ought to call your physician immediately to discover the relief that you require. He or she can provide supportive assistance that encompasses medication if he considers it necessary.

This additionally can be valuable in identifying mood swing patterns which could be a tool to long term treatment too.

Keep Your Physician Informed

Even though you might dislike going to the physician and you might believe that your physician never ever has anything desirable to say, it is extremely essential to keep him informed. By informing him of what is happening and how you are feeling, he could make better decisions.

You ought to call your physician:

- When you feel a mood swing is about occur at some point soon.

- when you feel that a mood swing is happening

- When your medications are not functioning as you believed they would.

- When you have any kind of suicidal ideas, sensations of despair or are having difficulty making it through the day without being sad.

When your loved ones inform you that you are undergoing a mood swing or they inform you that you are showing indications of either depressive signs or mania according to their understanding.

Your physician can assist you in finding out how to deal with these circumstances. They could additionally prescribe medication differences that could additionally serve as a tool for enhancing your well being and health.

By keeping your physician notified, you enable your signs to be monitored. Your physician can discover patterns and even discover the things that activate these episodes. That can result in benefits across your lifetime consisting of the avoidance of those scenarios which are going to cause fewer episodes across your lifetime.

Finding out how to deal with bipolar is a necessity. By having a look at your life today, you'll have the ability to see things that could be altered that are going to eventually enhance your wellness. Do you sleep well? Do you eat well? Do you understand what your early warning indications are? Taking care of these changes now is going to eventually enhance your general wellness.

You could discover how to manage bipolar. Now, there are a couple of more things you may do as well.

Chapter 6: Support Groups

Everybody dislikes them and not one person wishes to go to support groups. However, consider why that is. Is it too difficult to do? Do you dislike confessing that anything might be wrong? Maybe you are like one of the many who really find themselves dealing with the requirement to surround yourself with others who deal with the very same difficulties as you.

The bottom line is that support groups do assist and that they typically can assist in boosting your life quality and aiding you to recognize what you are dealing with.

Finding out how to manage bipolar is not easy; however, it is demanding. It is a thing that you can find out how to do. Actually, among the most effective methods to do this is to work with other people who are dealing with the identical circumstances that you are.

Support groups provide that kind of care, something that your friends and family are not able to offer you nor can your physician. Being around other people who are dealing with the same issues you are dealing with, offers you understanding, hope and even a feeling of calmness.

Finding out about support groups is critically vital. Who is in yours depends upon your family composition and even those who are making every effort to supply you with the care which you require.

Today, you most likely have a family that is aiding to support your requirements. You additionally have a healthcare team which exists to offer you with medical support. This consists of everybody from your family physician.

Buddies ought to comprise part of your support group as well. Many do not wish to supply individual information about themselves like their bipolar, however, the reality is that you ought to. A real buddy remains by you and helps you to cope in addition to offering you the support you require at all times.

Think about informing those that you love about what is taking place. It could just benefit you. What's more, it could assist folks to comprehend the manner in which you respond and the moods which you go through, turning you into a better buddy to them.

Outside Help

While having your family around you is going to enhance your wellbeing and is going to provide the assistance that you require, you ought to think about extra assistance through outside too.

Professional groups which meet to cover bipolar disorder are located in lots of recreation centers, hospitals and numerous psychiatric facilities. To discover one that is located close to you, ask your physician for recommendations. They might have one that is customized to your particular requirements.

These support groups offer expert attention that could be directed by you. For instance, a number of individuals that have the identical condition as you may come together with a mediator. By sharing the details of your day with other people, you aid them to enhance their life as much as you are going to help yourself to accomplish the identical thing.

Bipolar is a condition where isolation results in aggravating signs. A therapy group is going to supply you with the requirements that you have in meeting others who have your identical signs. It aids you to understand that others out there are undergoing the identical things as you. It is an exceptional assistance in recognizing that you aren't on your own in what you are dealing with.

If that is still insufficient to get you to a support group, the reality is that a number of those who do take part in them really discover a decrease in their signs! By having the ability to speak about your stresses and your issues, you boost the quantity of time in between your mood swing episodes.

Not just are you going to be receiving benefits from outside support group members, however you additionally offer them to others.

Nobody else can feel the irritation of feeling down and miserable and not understanding why. And, nobody else can comprehend completely the issues with taking meds and the outright reality that you'll deal with bipolar for the remainder of your life.

By using assistance from both your friends and family and support groups, you could acquire a degree of benefit and understanding. Bipolar might be holding you versus your will, however with support from outside sources, you are able to fight against the impact it has on your regular and future life.

Chapter 7: The Mood Chart

Dealing with bipolar is a thing that you ought to do in numerous methods. One of those methods, as we have gone over, consists of monitoring your signs. While we went over a number of reasons why you want to watch for the early bipolar symptoms and signs, it is additionally essential for you to notice how your treatment is working.

To keep track of your own bipolar treatment, you want to utilize a mood chart. There are numerous simple, beneficial and rather effective manners in which you can accomplish this. A mood chart aids you to track the manner in which you feel on any given day. By monitoring this, you may better notice the downs and ups of your condition.

Your physician might ask you to keep a mood chart particularly at the start of your treatment. However, it is ideal to carry on with it for the long term since it offers you, your family, your buddies and your physician with assistance in identifying mood change episodes. When all of these people can gather, you'll see exceptional benefits in your regular life.

A mood chart is a straightforward journal. You are going to utilize it to track your mood changes, your regular feelings, the things that you carry out and the manner in which you sleep. It is rather an effective instrument when used well. Here's what to incorporate in your mood chart:

1. The manner in which you feel that day, including any changes in feelings. If you get up in an excellent mood, record this. If later somebody agitates you, record this as well.

2. Your activities additionally require to be recorded. If you head to work, jot it down. If you choose to spend the day in bed, this has to be recorded as well. Having the ability to monitor the things that you do is going to assist you and your physician to identify triggers and to identify approaching extreme mood swings.

3. Sleep patterns are really crucial to the bipolar person. You ought to keep track of the changes

which take place in your sleeping due to the fact that it is going to set off differences in your general well being.

4. Medications and negative side effects ought to additionally be thought about daily. In case you take your meds and after an hour feel like you require a nap, this ought to be recorded. It is really essential to keep in mind to include alterations in your general reaction, too. If you start to have brand-new side effects or ones which are exacerbated, this has to be taken into consideration.

5. Life alterations and life occasions which are substantial ought to be noted. Often, the stresses at work or the death of a loved one could cause mood changes that could be serious.

Most days, you are going to record an ordinary day. Often times you will not have a great deal of details to include in your mood chart. Other times, however, you might discover the requirement to include lots of details.

There are a number of various kinds of charts on the market which could be rather helpful to you. Pick one that your physician tells you is the best option. It is going to eventually supply you with the ideal record of how to handle your mood swings by monitoring them.

In case you do not wish to do this on paper, you can create a virtual diary on a file which you have on your computer system as well. To keep in mind to do this tracking, merely take note of it the identical time every day, possibly after you enjoy a meal. Diarize it! You are going to be rewarded with the responses that you require for regular life management.

Concluding Chapter

Bipolar is a life long condition that impacts countless individuals every year. The majority of them go on to live happy and regular lives since they discover the coping skills they require to empower themselves.

You have a choice. You could select to live a complete and content life which makes you pleased by making sacrifices now or you may keep on making decisions which impact the quality of your life and those who you love. While the path to a better life could be one that is loaded with battles and frequently the sensation of having to give things up, it is one that is going to eventually award you with a healthier, longer life.

These coping techniques are simply the beginning of your journey. Quickly you'll have the ability to see the things that impact you yourself and you'll have the ability to rein them in. You could enhance your life quality by just handling these parts of it.

I hope that you enjoyed reading through this book and that you have found it useful. If you want to share your thoughts on this book, you can do so by leaving a review on the Amazon page. Have a great rest of the day.

Printed in Great Britain
by Amazon

23238678R00047